ANCHOR BOOKS

WHISPERED MEMORIES

Edited by

Heather Killingray

First published in Great Britain in 2003 by
ANCHOR BOOKS
Remus House,
Coltsfoot Drive,
Peterborough, PE2 9JX
Telephone (01733) 898102

All Rights Reserved

Copyright Contributors 2002

HB ISBN 1 84418 064 6
SB ISBN 1 84418 065 4

FOREWORD

Anchor Books is a small press, established in 1992, with the aim of promoting readable poetry to as wide an audience as possible.

We hope to establish an outlet for writers of poetry who may have struggled to see their work in print.

The poems presented here have been selected from many entries, and as always editing proved to be a difficult task.

I trust this selection will delight and please the authors and all those who enjoy reading poetry.

Heather Killingray
Editor

CONTENTS

Serenade	Elsa Ivor	1
The Dove	Sophie Long	2
Bestest Dream	Daniel White	3
On The Stony Wall	Alan Johnston	4
Behind Closed Doors	Doreen Lee	5
Unread	Cynthia Taylor	6
I Don't Know	Derek William Gresty	7
April 2002	Joan Fletcher	8
Karen	Denis Rae	9
Love	Carole Mitchell	10
My Promise	Michala Cushen	11
I'm Coming Home	Mike Hain	12
Poles Apart	Steve J Waterfield	13
You And Me	Olive Hudson	14
My Darling Bride	Janet Cavill	15
My Love	Sharon Mary Birch	16
What Is Love?	Corinna Mangham	18
Just Because	J Winwood	19
Have You The Feeling?	Keith L Powell	20
Secret Love	Polina Belle McCann	21
Living Without You	Evelyn A Evans	22
A Valentine Wish	M Porter	24
The Smile Of Love	Charli Price	25
Lost Love	May Ward	26
Cloak Of Love	Hazel Mills	27
Remembering	E Evans	28
What Is Love?	Coleen Bradshaw	29
Old Love - New Love	George S Johnstone	30
Whispered Blessings	Alistair Gorringe	31
In Perfect Love	Meg Akusika Millar	32
You Flirt And Tantalise My Soul	David Catherall	33
For You	Kaz	34
My First Love	Tony Fuller	35
Love Hurts	Garry Knowles	36
The Silence Of Barkingside	Keith Leese	37
Never	Bernadette Mottram	38

Love Is . . .	Warren William Brown	39
Discovery	Clive Cornwall	40
I Still Do Love You	Parveen K Saini	41
Drama Of Love	Phil McLynn	42
Love Is	Andrew Pitcher	43
Are You Real?	Lance Honour	44
Love	W A Dean	45
Love	Frank Osborne	46
The One	Paul Stevenson	47
There's Always Me	Tracy Mitchell	48
The Sea Of Love	M Dawson	49
Loved Ones	Zynab Maria Al-Kadhim	50
Just You!	Elaine Hind	51
Soulmates	Rosalind Wood	52
The Dreamer	A R Bell	53
Seasons Of Love	Adrian Hill	54
Special Love	Julie Hampson	55
Love Is A Many-Splendoured Thing	Patricia Hunt	56
The Long Road	Angela Burse	57
Holding Love Inside	I M Stead	58
My Bob	Johnie Pruden	59
Best Of British	Fine Buliciri	60
The Queen Mother	P Evans	62
The Brightest Light	S M Wilkinson	63
Reflections On The Queen Mother At The Lying-In-State	Mollie D Earl	64
My Father	Terry Daley	66
March 10th	Anne Davey	67
My Special Friend	Diana Daley	68
Spirits Live On	Laura Linfield-Brown	69
My Dad	Marion Healy	70
My Loving Bride	Eamon John A Healy	71
A Golden Jubilee Riddle	Joyce Dawn Willis	72
Mother's Day	Sue Wichman	73
Bob	Betty Buckle	74
Mum	Margaret Thomas	75
My Husband, Roy	Celia Taylor	76

For David My Son	Doreen Walters	77
Ben	Elaine Chaplin	78
Daughters Of Mine	Steve Myers	80
There Are Angels	A C Dancer	82
A Mighty Man	Steven Hunter	83
My Son	K Vaughan	84
We Will Remember Them	Peggy Johnson	85
My Grandparents (1999)	Laura Somerville	86
My Mother	Betty Mai Challinor	87
Over The Rainbow	Kelly Pidwell	88
A Mother	John L Wright	89
Best Friend	Laura O'Rourke	90
Together Forever	Sheila Buckingham	91
Ruby Wedding Anniversary	Peter Englefield	92
My Most Precious Friend	Sue Starling	93
Lean On Me	Lin Sullivan	94
Michael Apollo Ronan Chakotay Knight	Michelle Knight	95
Grandad Ted	Tash Bazley	96
Open Up	Jayne Poulter	98

SERENADE

The summer evening stirs and sighs -
Brushing the coloured dream from the eyes,
And then the lovely night awakes -
The dark flower on the sunset shakes;
The twilight players have come late,
People on dark verandas wait
Hushed, for the first strains of the lute -
A serenade - but night is mute,
The scene for tender love is set,
Romeo climbs to Juliet
This very night, yet gone afar
As that small reproachful star -
And people sigh, because they are
Too tired for music, and instead
Sleep the bereft sleep of the dead.

Elsa Ivor

THE DOVE

The graceful dove
As white as snow
The feeling of love
She does not know
The dove wakes early
She cannot sleep
She looks into the distance
At the sea so deep
She longs to be held
By the sun in the sky
Someone to help her
Hold her head high
Touched by the sun
She begins to sing
And flies into the distance
The sun at her wing.

Sophie Long

BESTEST DREAM

(Dedicated to Eileen Regan, course tutor for counselling skills and those met on course)

Memories of the smiles left behind
What a simple message to give,
a message of liking and acceptance
'Thank you, I am glad I met you'
If a smile could speak, that's what it would say
Memories of how we cared and shared,
of hearts that shone like a summer's day.
We worked together like a team,
just like the bestest dream.

Daniel White

ON THE STONY WALL

There is a stony wall
When a was a boy
That was green wi moss
That was grey wi dust

Doon the winding path
Overgrown wi gress
Doon beside the burn
That a liked the best

A wis young and daft
You wir younger yit
Efter school ad walk
That is where wi met

A wid hud yer hand
Your wee yin in mine
Your hair wis long and black
Your eyes wid shine

We loved each ither we said
We said we always wid
Noo wir auld an grey
Am gled wi did.

Alan Johnston

BEHIND CLOSED DOORS

The secret side of someone you love
Heartache and pain no one can disprove
Workaholic with an obsession for wealth
Foregoing all pleasures, putting a strain on one's health.
In public a devoted person is how they seem
But behind closed doors the violence begins
With nowhere to hide from the punches and blows
The suffering and pain no one ever knows
Why do they change, nobody seems to understand
Is it a mental pressure or is it all planned?
After it's over, apologies and regret
How can they be so different from when you first met?
The love that was shared as years roll by.
Now the satisfaction they get seeing you cry.
Promises they make that it will never happen again
Can never erase the heartache and pain.
Why do we stay with someone so unkind?
But it's hard to go and leave your whole life behind.
It's foolish to stay, but hard to go.
The truth if it's known, that you still love him so.

Doreen Lee

UNREAD

Returned unopened the envelope said,
Weeping - my heart echoed - *Unread.*
Unread the nights of shattering pain -
The awful fear of never seeing *you* again -
Unread the laughter - the fun that we shared,
The times we acknowledged - how *much* we cared.
Unread the days - as our love grew,
The limitless joy - of me, and you.
All that we did, and all that we said, *Unread!*

Cynthia Taylor

I DON'T KNOW

How deep is deep in my heart
How long is eternity
How far is miles apart?
Who knows, what will be will be.

Will everything come if I wait
Will my eyes show my feelings inside
Shall I stand up and shout, let me feelings out
Or not, and be slave to my pride?

Derek William Gresty

APRIL 2002

How good it feels to walk again,
Instead of rushing from the rain,
How good to breathe the April air
And feel the sun upon your hair,
The daffodils are fading now
How much we love their golden show
And in their wake a myriad blooms
With colours bright and sweet perfumes
Camellias, pink in great profusion
Their velvet petals no illusion
And small and sweet in many hues
The lovely polyanthus blooms
The cabbage-white is hov'ring there
Looking out for the buddleia
The blackbird calling from above
Come build a nest with me my love
And we will fly to paradise
For spring is here, and love's so nice.

Joan Fletcher

KAREN

A few months ago when we first met
And started chatting on the internet
Neither of us knew then how clear
A relationship would become so dear
Our closeness became of one mind
Forever amazed to always find
Both our senses recently have thrived
Spirits and angels just contrived
To bring us together for one reason
Our lives meant for many a season
Karen, you are the one for me
It has become so easy to see
Why you are the chosen one
Our life together has only begun.

Denis Rae

LOVE

What is this love inside of me
Which overwhelms me so?
And yet it brings a fear with it
But still it continues to grow

This love I feel, so overwhelming
Does surely pain my heart,
But it also brings to me
An ecstasy apart.

It is a love which has no end
Nor even a beginning
It grew from nothing
But now it does
Fill my very being.

Carole Mitchell

MY PROMISE
(For my sweetness darling)

I promise to love you always,
And give my heart to you.
I promise to be there for you,
And give my life to you.

I don't ever want that feeling,
Of not having you there.
I never want it in my mind,
It's a feeling I could not bear.

I love you more than ever,
Please believe it's true.
I can't think of anything better,
Than spending my whole life with you.

Michala Cushen

I'M COMING HOME

The desert night is my only friend,
The mountain roads never seem to end,
Strong black coffee to wake me up,
No one but me and my trusted old truck.
My dashboard holds an old picture of us,
It's time to roll, it's nearly dusk.
Our favourite song plays all night,
I coming to you cos I know it's right.

I'm coming home to face the truth,
To my small-town girl I don't want to lose.
The open road is no place to be,
Just sorry it took three years to see.
But a man needs time to sort himself out,
And now I'm done I have no doubts.
Spent enough time hurting alone,
I'm turning round - I'm coming home.

It's been three years since I saw you last,
Had to be strong and face the past.
Had a burning desire to call you each day,
But I knew it was best to stay away.
The past three years have been tough to face,
A stranger about town in a foreign place.
No more empty whiskey bottles as I'm feeling in control,
Baby, hold on - I'm coming home.

I heard last week that we have a child,
And as I drove, I just broke down and cried.
The fears I had inside are gone,
I just want you back, it's been so long.
I want to be there to see our child grow,
Baby, hold on - I'm coming home.

Mike Hain

POLES APART

You stir not to the rapture of my strings,
nor dwell spellbound on what enchants my sight.
The blissful word that lends my spirit wings,
leaves you unmoved, or wins your playful slight.
But when your circle's little twists of fate
wring out your tears, my eyes remain unproved.
And when life's petty doings you relate,
my distant stare betrays a mind removed.
Truly our stars ascend in different spheres,
to rise and rest at distant poles apart.
Then, love, what is this magic that endears
and subjugates the nature to the heart?
Who knows? But may its mysteries endure,
to sow this sweet confusion evermore.

Steve J Waterfield

YOU AND ME

Oh where shall I begin?
I love you my darling although you don't know,
The mother of my grandchildren, whom I love so.
Your qualities I admire, so rich and so pure,
You're strong and assured, a mind of your own,
I've waited so long for a daughter, you know,
Never thought it would be, I felt so alone,
When you came along just like a breeze
I grabbed you with joy, I fell to my knees,
Thank you my darling, I love you so,
You make my son happy, that's all I know.

Olive Hudson

MY DARLING BRIDE

Come with me my loved *one*
To land so far away
I'll get to know you loved *one*
And bear you on our way.

Today we'll go to *Cornwall*
St Ives, to be precise
You are so fair my *Idwall*
My one true paradise.

You are my Rose of *Sharon*
My lily - oh so sweet
Your hair so sweet *auburn*
Our lives together meet.

Today we stood before God's *altar*
We must never, never *falter.*

Janet Cavill

MY LOVE

The mirror shows me a reflection
But my eyes show me the night.
Whence comes this self-rejection?
And who switched off my light?

As a voice unheard says, 'Look again'
I have no strength to face this pain.

So I turn away from me
And my foot is forced to step.
My faithless eyes no longer see.
I stumble, soulless and bereft.

And a voice ignored sighs, 'Please turn back'
But my night turns from grey to black.

So I journey far and wide
Seeking sunshine; fleeing dark.
I think about a life,
Rejecting feelings and my heart.

Please listen love, is there a whisper on the breeze?
But such feelings so elusive, they slip away from me.

As I travel ever on
The sun casts shadows in my soul,
So I force my foot to turn,
Pleading, 'Someone make me whole.'

And a whisper growing louder, tells me I have a choice,
And my soul begins to listen to that ever kinder voice.

I face the darkness and the pain,
Inviting shadows now to leave.
And it is thus that I discover
My love; I journey into *me.*

Dancing on the breeze, a voice cries joyfully.
I can listen; I can hear it, it's my *voice, loving* me.

Sharon Mary Birch

WHAT IS LOVE?

Love is when He sits with me and cries,
Love is when He helps me through those tough goodbyes,
Love is the pain He endures for me,
Love is knowing He will never leave.

Love is His support, His listening ears,
Love is His teachings throughout the years,
Love is the joy, the miracles He makes,
Love is the strength that He fills within me.

Love is the warmth I feel when He's near,
Love is His forgiveness for all my sins,
Love is the ability to speak what I feel,
Love is not giving up on me after all these years.

What is love?
God is love.

Corinna Mangham

JUST BECAUSE

Because you mean the world to me
and bring me joy each day
Because you make my sun to shine
in your own kind of way
Because you drive dark clouds away
and bring me skies of blue
Because when rainbows show a face
it's just because of you

Because my life is dark and drear
when you are not around
Because my life is in your hands
then happiness I've found
Because you show me quiet peace
with things you say and do
Because you give me thoughts of love
so I realise - anew

That prayers and dreams sometimes come true
Because, because of you.

J Winwood

HAVE YOU THE FEELING?

Have you the feeling I have for you?
Then dance again with me please, please will you?
So that I can hold you close
More and more throughout the night.

Have you the feeling I have for you?
Deep down inside your heart, oh yes,
How can I put it to the test
More and more throughout the night?

Have you the feeling I have for you?
Then let us run away right now
There is a way, I am sure, oh somehow
More and more throughout the night.

Keith L Powell

SECRET LOVE

Across the room our glances met
Deeply into your eyes I gazed
Seeing the love for me you held
That neither time nor distance could erase.
Still I knew that we must part
Your tender kisses I would no more receive.
Love for you would stay deep in my heart
Though your loving caresses I would not feel.

I pass you by whene'er we meet
I look at you but dare not greet.
We who shared such tender feelings
We pass as strangers in the street.

Polina Belle McCann

Living Without You

As I sit alone today
I feel you close and near
But instead of feeling comforted
I want to shed a tear
If only you could be here
To share my life today
I would feel much better
In a happy loving way
I know this cannot be
As I feel nostalgic and alone
My life will never be the same
Without you in the home
Did you know how much I loved you?
I never told you so
I just got happily on with life
But I guess you knew and know
I never envisaged being alone
I thought it would happen never
Just getting on with daily life
Forever and forever
I treasure the moments I feel you near
Even though it makes me sad
I recall the things we did together
Tell myself I should be glad
Draw close to me and be near me oft
It is all that I have left
Of all the days that used to be
Before I was left bereft
It is hard to come to terms with
With all the things I do
Doing things just for me
Because I did them all for you

I am broken-hearted
I know it will never mend
Until we are together
When my life here on Earth will end
As the years go rolling by
I will always feel the same
Reminiscing, missing you
Desperately calling out your name.

Evelyn A Evans

A Valentine Wish

Another year older
I'm still feeling blue
Pining and dreaming
And thinking of you.

What can I say?
My name not betray
My thoughts are of you
On Valentine's Day.

I know you won't come
To my door late at night
Clutching a box of Turkish Delight
Or even a bottle of fruit of the vine
Inviting me out to wine and to dine.

Still - never mind, I'm not free anyway
We'll have to make it some other day.

M Porter

THE SMILE OF LOVE

I used to not believe
That real love could be true
But now I start to question
What I thought I knew
Because every time I'm with you
My heart seems to slowly melt
My eyes are full of wonder
Because this feeling I've never felt
And now we are together
Nothing can wipe my smile
I need to get used to this feeling
And that might take me a while
When I'm all alone
You're the only thing on my mind
This love is the feeling
I always dreamt I might find!

Charli Price

LOST LOVE

When we parted I felt sad,
It almost broke my heart,
You were tall and handsome, loving and caring,
A happy life together we could have been sharing.

When I first met you I never knew,
That I would fall in love with you,
But I know now it could never be,
Not for you or for me.

There is one thing no one can ever do,
Is to take away those loving memories of you,
So nice to have loved, laughed, and cried,
All I have left are a few souvenirs that with me bide.

May Ward

CLOAK OF LOVE

Enfold me in your great cloak of love,
Warm and soft, with its velvet hood;
Holding me safe and so close to you;
Bind us together in midnight blue.

Enfold me beneath the pale moonlight,
Where shimmering stars do shine so bright.
Let your sweet love drift gently o'er me,
Raising my hopes and setting me free.

Enfold me through the darkest of nights,
Bringing to me the brightest of lights;
Casting their glow on our love so true,
Drape o'er me your soft cloak of blue.

Enfold me now 'til the end of time
And I'll gather the stars and make them thine.
The moon I will catch to be your plaything
And I'll give unto you a bright golden ring.

Hazel Mills

REMEMBERING

I still remember
why should I forget?
Those happier days
when we first met.

Before the laughter
turned to cold
bitter tears
to the pain of my fears.

Memories of the joy
of your warm embrace
the soft sweet kisses
rained on your face.

I still remember
though remember alone
what we could be now
if our love still shone.

E Evans

WHAT IS LOVE?

What is Love?
It is something that God has sent from above
And is in association with the dove
Which is always on the move

What is Love?
When a man and his wife
Stay together for life
As husband and strife

What is Love?
It's when a dog wags its tail
And knows you will not fail
For they can smell a left-behind trail

What is Love?
When people kiss
Then make a wish
For this is bliss.

What is Love?
It's when two people say 'I do'
Then say 'I love you.'

Coleen Bradshaw

OLD LOVE - NEW LOVE

When love gathers dust in the corner
Take time to search your soul again,
Ennui and monotony have become embittered
A heavy load shackled by a rusty chain.

When love no longer seems quite appealing
In the lives you exist but only just,
Moving on appears the sensible option
There's little point in dwelling around mistrust.

When love has faded like your last dream
You linger in a world of yesterday,
But the pain of losing that reality
Makes you feel humble in every way.

When love hastens arrows from Cupid's bow
There's no guarantee it'll find your heart,
Only if you were as lucky as I was
The solitude abates with a fresh start.

When love grants you a second chance
Seize that opportunity, hold her tight,
For each moment is precious with love anew
Guide it forward gently, keep it in sight.

When love has found that fresh beginning
Two people can bridge that emotional link,
Share thoughts in silence, but each knowing
It need not be written down in ink.

George S Johnstone

WHISPERED BLESSINGS

Painting autumn leaves in dreams
Upon your back my brush is sweeping
Beside the singing golden stream
Whispered dreams worth keeping

Above our bodies the sisken sings
Far from land which man devours
Born of love on silver wings
And laced with sunlit flowers

We who talk in break of morning
Laid beside the tallest trees
Above us sunlight may be dawning
A summer sky or winter freeze

In bliss we stay there waiting still
Love breathes her sigh of sighs
We who climbed the distant hills
Are lost in swirling ocean tides

Upon my finger the needles wound
In freely-flowing forest calm
To bless a love that nature found
Your cheek pressed to my palm

Enchanting leaves lie all around,
As we sit amidst the silent bliss
And in my heart I hear your sound
Then feel it with a kiss

A woodland kiss so soft and free
We laugh in stories often sung
Together under fairest trees
Whispered blessings in the young.

Alistair Gorringe

IN PERFECT LOVE

Whenever your goals are overshadowed by fear,
Remember there is hope
Whenever your faith is weakened by fear
Remember there is light
When your voice is lost and your heart becomes cold,
When reassurance and inspiration needed
Close your eyes and feel your strength
Remember the essence of life,
Love in its perfection.
When you open your eyes again
You will see the world in a different shade
You will know that you are not alone
You will believe then,
That perfect love is the essence of life.

Meg Akusika Millar

YOU FLIRT AND TANTALISE MY SOUL

I long to gaze within your eyes,
And hear the sound of your tender sighs,
As we talk and as we speak
I long to kiss you on the cheek.

Your winning smile and knowing grin,
That pleasure comes from deep within,
You flatter me with what you say,
And dispel my fears in disarray.

How I long that I might kiss your lips,
Like nectar sweet, with longing sips,
To know the thoughts within your head,
Would lead me to my lover's bed,

I know your love, it has control,
It satisfies both body and soul,
In my thoughts you'll always be,
Now and for eternity.

You flirt and tantalise my soul,
With little white lies, I'd lose control,
But gently you lead the way,
And hold my love, so it will stay.

Within your arms I long to be,
Safe and secure for eternity,
And when my night it turns to day,
I know your love, won't slip away.

David Catherall

FOR YOU

Although we're not together
And we can never be,
Each night while I am sleeping
I feel you here with me.

The distances between us
Are more than simply miles.
I have to look at pictures
To see one of your smiles.

I ask you questions daily,
But you don't say a word.
My heart tells me your answers,
That silent prayers you've heard.

Our lives are just too different,
They keep us far apart.
Still you have a special place
So deep within my heart.

I know I've found my soulmate,
Of that I am quite sure,
Though I know we cannot be,
I'll love you evermore.

Kaz

My First Love

I fell in love when first we met, when I was just fifteen.
I loved you then, I love you still, and all the years between.
I left my home, was all alone, in oh, so many ways!
That memory warm, helped smooth my path
throughout those lonely days.
Now I am old, way past my prime, with hair that's turning white.
The memory of my first young love still reaches me at night.
And though I love another now from whom I'll never part.
My first young love will always have a corner of my heart.

Tony Fuller

LOVE HURTS

To answer the question of 'What is love?'
There's only one simple reply.
Some will just smile - the know-it-alls.
Then procrastinate till they've thought of a lie.

To me love comes in all special casts.
In shapes and in all different sizes.
Not always physical, like human to human.
But sometimes objects in cherished disguises.

It's not always things you can actually see.
Some will give their love to the Lord.
Whilst others love the theatre and sit all bewitched.
Showing their love in the form of applaud.

Some love their pets, sailing, their house.
Their car, computer, music or bike.
Love's not confined to just we mere mortals.
In reality you can love what you like.

But whatever you love the feeling's the same.
A glow that grows deep inside.
A wanting, a need, a passion to contain.
Whether objects or person or spiritual guide.

But there's one thing for sure, love always hurts.
Like a pet that will suddenly die.
Your heart will be broken, ripped from your chest.
Leaving you empty and helpless to cry.

So to answer the question, 'What is love?'
Be confident and show no alarm.
Reply quite simply with the following words.
Love is ill-treatment, dis-service and harm.

Garry Knowles

THE SILENCE OF BARKINGSIDE
(The twenty-fifth anniversary edition)

Pretending to feel no more than good friends we parted,
a farewell drink, but why did we feel so down-hearted?
Too afraid to speak of love, we imprisoned our fate,
love seemed so impossible in that year of seventy-eight.

Pretending to feel no more than good friends we kissed,
farewell tidings, yet not a word of love or being missed.
Too afraid to speak of sorrow, made silent this goodbye,
but on leaving Barkingside, did I see a tear fill your eye?

Pretending to feel no more than good friends we waved,
hundreds of miles must part us, and love's call betrayed.
Too afraid to speak of passion, forged this last farewell,
until the silence of Barkingside, finds voice in us to tell.

Keith Leese

NEVER

I never meant to fall in love
Never meant to fall so hard
Never thought it possible
After all the tears and scars

But was I such a stupid fool
To believe in all you said
To tell you all my secrets
And let you inside my head?

Not just my head, my heart as well
You broke down that wall of ice
I put it there to protect myself
And to keep me safe and wise

But against my better judgement
My heart and soul you won
And before I knew what hit me
My self-control was gone

I never meant to fall in love
And I never will again
I never want to hurt like this
I never want to feel such pain.

Bernadette Mottram

LOVE IS...

Love is a creased face
Where only a tear may roll.
Love is a huge expansive place
Which opens your very soul
Love is a mind full of games
Where there are no competitive winners
Love it so mercilessly shames
The accomplice and the sinners
Love, the greatest expectation
To all who lay before
Love this world of elation
Where everyone interprets the score
Love's a crime for the youth
Yet fruitless for the blundering fool
Love is confronting the truth
Because love will conquer all.

Warren William Brown

DISCOVERY

Each thing discovered with you I hold dear
New feelings, new worlds, new places, new life
Memories, many ever more valuable than gold.
Experiences and little things too I'll always hold
Scents and sounds and sights and times of laughter.
Tears too, some sad and some happy but all shared
Sharing the rock and sand of a mystical Cornwall
The delight of Suffolk and the vine of Kent
Magical spell of the Cotswolds and the love of Essex.

Clive Cornwall

I STILL DO LOVE YOU

We both were strongly bonded together.
We made decisions together and were willing to challenge the world,
But this illness of yours has put a stop to many things.
Don't get me wrong, I have not given up.
It's just sometimes I feel alone.
All decisions and challenges I face today.
I must say your illness brings the worst in me.
I can see the frustration in you.
You want to be independent and free,
But how is it possible?
Your pain seems unbearable at times.
I hear you night and day calling me to help you in a
                                      peaceful death today.
I can't do it,
Even if illness has over come you.
I still do love you.

Parveen K Saini

DRAMA OF LOVE

He sold his business building boats in Marlow
And bought a busy bar in St Malo
Where English tourists spend money like water
So it's private schools for his son and daughter

And you'd think with this and a house he rented
That he would be happy and contented
But his wife whom he loved died ten years ago
And loneliness is falling like harsh winter snow

So he hopes one day he'll find a wife
We all need a special light in our life
And though he's always avoided the losers
He's been hurt twice by crafty users

He sips Coke in the bar, surrounded by boozers
And sailors on leave from their battle cruisers
Sometimes alone he'll have a quiet sob
But a woman of thirty asks for a job

And though he's fifty she is attracted
So now their drama of love is enacted
And the days are gone, when he used to feel low
And loneliness fell like harsh winter snow.

Phil McLynn

LOVE IS

When first in love, you'll start to sing,
Smile a lot and give her everything.
The courting starts, the race begun,
With hours of pleasure, and lots of fun.
All because there's not enough to do,
To show her that your love is true.
And when you see your friends, you would say,
'She's the best, that's ever come my way.'

There's gifts of chocolates, bunches of flowers,
All to show her, that your love never sours.
Treats for her, forever going out,
At the movies or pub, it's always your shout.

Then as time passes by, the fire dies down,
You're always out, with the boys 'on the town'.
Call her sometimes, when you care to choose,
Because it's comfortable now, like a pair of old shoes.
The gifts, they've gone, the treats are few,
Now she's something that isn't new.

And it all comes to an end, and you don't know why,
It's because of you! So don't dare cry.

Andrew Pitcher

ARE YOU REAL?

Sometimes I think I hear your voice,
Then I think I see your face,
But I awaken from my reverie,
And you're gone without a trace.

I look around for signs,
That you were not just a dream,
But there's just a room that's empty,
No love passed this way, it seems.

Has fantasy run away with me?
Or do you exist for real?
If you do then please just show me,
For you have a tortured heart to heal.

Lance Honour

LOVE

Love has been a mystery through the ages
First it simmers and then it rages
If you're lucky it returns to a simmer
If you're not it begins to get dimmer
Finally familiarity breeds contempt
Love gave up and off it went
Was it love anyway or just lust?
Physical attraction sure to go bust
Good whilst it lasted but too shallow to succeed
A tasty snack but nothing else on which to feed
Is it better to have loved and lost than never to have loved at all?
Or should you have stayed at home and never gone to the ball?

Unrequited love has a pain of its own
Unreturned feelings and being alone
But many partners become just as lonely
Feelings dead, not even homely
Have your dreams and enjoy love when it next comes around
Experience the highs but be ready to come back down to the ground
It's your choice, no one can advise
I simply offer a word to the wise
Enjoy the buzz, the warmth and the gloss
But be prepared for the pain and the loss.

W A Dean

LOVE

Love has no need of words at all
When on that fateful day you fall
Your heart just stops, then starts again
Then skips a beat to ascertain
If this is real or just a dream
Or merely thoughts of self-esteem
And why my heart should feel this way
It wasn't like this yesterday
And should I try to reason why
December now seems warm July
Oh no my love, let's not entreat
Why love makes two hearts so complete
Those lonely nights when you're away
That leaves my world in disarray
But sleep won't come although I try
Just dreams of love to vivify
In loneliness I'm left to yearn
To hold you close when you return
And take you in my arms and pray
My life is spent with you each day.

Frank Osborne

THE ONE

Just when you think your last chance has gone
In walks a girl so beautiful, could this be 'the one'?
She smiles like an angel, and looks like one too
Is it possible, could this be, will she fall for you?

There is something about her that I really love
Like a valley so deep and the mountains above
She makes me feel happy, she's so gentle and kind
Do you think she might, you know, some time end up being mine?

I love her so much with all of my heart
So many good points, so where do I start?
She's special, she's sexy, she's gorgeous, she's kind
She's amazing, she's lovely, I hope she'll be mine

She will always be there in times of despair
She's supportive, she's helpful, she's brilliant, she'll care
She makes me feel happy in my times of sadness
She'll stand by me in my times of madness

I couldn't have wished for a girl much better
I'm so glad, so really really glad that I met her
It's true and I hope you all believe
The best day of my life was definitely on Christmas Eve

We'll have many good times; we'll have a few bad
I will make you happy but, no doubt, sometimes sad
I only hope the tears you cry are of joy and laughter
I will endeavour to do my best for you, past, present and hereafter

My girlfriend, I love you with all of my heart
My girlfriend, I hope that we never ever part
My girlfriend, my darling, two years have fast gone
My girlfriend, my darling, I want to be your 'one'.

Paul Stevenson

THERE'S ALWAYS ME

Always the one to count on
I'll be the one to care
Don't worry if things should go wrong
You know I'll be there.
If you want to hurt someone's feelings
I'm here, pick on me; I'll keep smiling
Anyway, through my tears I can see
I don't expect any praise, for things
I may have done, just keep on reminding me
Of all the things I did wrong.
Don't worry, I don't need love or for you
To tell me you care: if you have any hurt
To give, you know I'm always there.
I wonder if one day you'll realise
The pain you put me through, if that day
Should ever come, will I still be here
Waiting alone for you?

Tracy Mitchell

THE SEA OF LOVE

They told me time would heal the pain
I answered them 'Not so.'
They told me joy would come again.
How could they ever know
How great my grief, how deep my love?
It never could be true
That joy would ever come again
Unless it came with you.

Without you Dear, I did endure,
My heart it did survive
This malady without a cure,
The pain kept me alive.

Then a wise one said to me
'Consider if you will
If you should cry into the sea
It would not overspill.
The sea of Love is vast and deep
A mighty rolling ocean,
A billion tears into it weep
It will not change its motion.'

And so my Love without a tear
I face the new tomorrow.
The joy we shared when you were here
Outmeasures far my sorrow.

M Dawson

LOVED ONES

Look inside a book, it says:
Who cares for you these days?
Who has the gift of making much,
From everything they hold or touch?
Who by a wave of a hand,
Draws ships from foreign lands?
Who guards you in the dark of night,
And in the morning sends you light?
Who comes to you to say,
'Thank you for your love today'?
Who holds you close to their heart,
And thinks of you when you're apart?
Who helps you when you are in trouble,
And takes you out of a bursting bubble?
Who in your life plays a key role,
And is always your famous hero?
Who gives you all their hearts' force?
Your parents of course.

Zynab Maria Al-Kadhim

JUST YOU!
(For Martin - who turned my heart around)

I would travel across broken glass, just to hold your hand.
I would write your name forever, in the softly-graded sand.
I would stay awake, eternally, just to watch you by my side.
I would starve all purpose, just to see you take a stride.
I would shield you from elements, that suddenly made you cold.
I would fall from any height, so long as you were always there to hold.
I would become your protector, so I always catch your pain.
I would create your destiny, so all there is, is gain.
I would salute your heart, so it knows which way to go.
I would easily say 'I love you' so for sure you'll always know.
I would here, now, and tomorrow, be all you ever need.
I would never show you dishonesty, and definitely never greed.
I would savour my last breath, and keep it safely just for you.
I would consider you perfect, refreshing and something
                                                        completely new.
I would grace you for all the time ahead and more.
I would greet you with an embrace each time you enter the door.
I would fold you in my arms and feel the follow flow
I would become dead inside, should you ever . . . decide to go.

Elaine Hind

SOULMATES

For everlasting love
to 'touch' your life
and through the
'Eyes of God'
become
Man and Wife

Is a blessing bestowed
on a
'chosen' few
and this
'gift'
has been given to
each of you

So live for the moment
Time cannot be measured
Forever is now
Each day to be treasured

For as 'soulmates' together
You never will part
Your love will always
be alive in your hearts.

Rosalind Wood

THE DREAMER

Our eyes met, at the dance
I knew she was the one
A lovely girl, so full of fun
A girl I had met, just by chance

We danced, and talked, all through the night
We didn't want to part
Her looks, her smile, captured my heart
Our future looked so bright.

I took her home, and held her tight
I felt her beating heart
We kissed tenderly, at the start
I held her close, it seemed so right.

My heart was racing madly
My kisses covered her face
- Her neck, and every possible place
We were lost in passion - but sadly

The alarm clock, rang, loud and clear
I had to get out of bed
Why, oh why - had my love fled
When we had found, a love so rare?

Maybe things will be alright
She is too lovely to forget
Maybe - it's not over yet
I'll see her, in my dream tonight.

A R Bell

SEASONS OF LOVE

In the brightest light of day
I have an easy mind
For I have you forever
But let me once remind

In the hopeful breath of spring
Where nothing is ever slow
We met as fate had ordered
I know our love will grow

In the heart of blazing summer
When skies sing out so blue
I look at you with wonder
I know our love is true

In the blustery winds of autumn
Golden leaves begin to fall
But I can smile securely
I know our love won't pall

In the bleakest days of winter
Seared by blinding cold
Still I feel contented
I know our love will hold

In the darkest hours past midnight
Your heart beats close to mine
We lie in blissful slumber
Our bodies still entwined.

Adrian Hill

SPECIAL LOVE

I wished for an angel
Then you came to me
And filled my life with happiness
And let my soul be free
You filled an empty space
No one else could see
And created a special love
The one for you and me.

When I prayed for a miracle
That's when I found you
And now I've given my heart
My dreams can now come true
Someone to share the good times
And help each other through bad
To hold each other near
When life seems lonely and sad

When I asked for love
That's when you found me
And a life together
We can share, you'll see
The nights won't seem so long
And the days will go so fast
For a special love
One that's made to last.

Julie Hampson

LOVE IS A MANY-SPLENDOURED THING

'Love' is a many-splendoured thing!
The warmth of your smile,
Is all worthwhile,
And to hold your hand,
Gives me a very warm glow!
Your kiss I feel is very sincere,
I'm beginning to wonder if I'm still here!
I've had my daydreams and dizzy spells
'Is this love?' I ask myself
My thumping heart tells me so!
With the feeling of fire and a wonderful glow
This 'love' does feel a wonderful thing!
I think of all the 'happiness' it could bring.
'Love is a many-splendoured thing.'

Patricia Hunt

THE LONG ROAD

The journey has been long and hard, a struggle to the end,
But I'm glad we walked together, hand-in-hand, my friend.
We've reached the end of the road now; I really cannot stay,
And yet I cannot leave you, to go my lonely way.
You are a part of me, a part I won't deny,
I won't ever forget you; I don't even want to try.
Yet the road divides now, and my road isn't yours,
And still I linger, waiting, a silent little pause.
I must not stay. I won't look back. The only way is on,
You'll always be in my heart, that joyful little song.
Don't be sad. Don't look back. Be glad for all we shared.
If you ever retrace your steps, remember that I cared.
I know that as time passes, you'll forget me, we both know it's true!
The same can't be said of me. How could I forget you?
The time we had was poignant, truly bittersweet,
I don't regret our journey, and I'm glad our paths did meet.
So, carry on with your travels, and I'll go on with mine.
I will survive, all thanks to you, I know now I'll be fine.

Angela Burse

HOLDING LOVE INSIDE

I don't tell how I love you much,
And how proud I stand each day.
But inside love overflows,
And this is just my way.

I look on you as my closest friend,
One who's always there for me.
As tall I stand with a mother's pride,
For the entire world to see.

So know how much I love you,
As this love grows with each day.
And just speaking as your mother
I feel proud and oh, so lucky!
That you were sent my way.

I M Stead

MY BOB
(A tribute on behalf of my lovely cousin, Maisie, for her beloved husband Bob)

An angel smiled at Bob
As he entered Heaven's gate
'Come in dear, we need you here
We're glad that you're not late.

An organiser is what we need
One that knows the lingo
You certainly fill the bill
We want you to teach us bingo!'

Bob smiled a nervous smile
Turned to the angel and said,
'Thanks for your wonderful welcome
I've just left my loved ones for a while.'

'Fear not,' said the angel,
'You have earned your rest,
For whilst on Mother Earth,
You were just simply the best!'

Johnie Pruden

BEST OF BRITISH
(A tribute for the Golden Jubilee)

An adventurous journey up 'north', with Alan Bennett,
a newspaper covering fish and chips,
hours of laughter with 'Carry on' films,
Brighton and Blackpool, seaside family summer trips.
That's what I love about being British.

The Royal family,
A national and international treasure,
Alexander McQueen and Stella McCartney,
hip English fashion, made to measure.
That's what I love about being British.

The Houses of Parliament, the Tower of London,
                               and Buckingham Palace,
architectural and historical relics, a joy to behold
                               within this nation state,
theatrical arts and talent unrivalled anywhere,
'Harry Potter' our latest literary hero of late.
That's what I love about being British.

The Lake District and the Isle of Wight,
two picturesque landscapes for one to behold,
St George and the Dragon,
the most heroic story ever told.
that's what I love about being British.

A sense of fair play,
the 'Bulldog' fighting spirit, when all appears lost,
respect for the underdog,
the Falklands war, heroically fought at all cost.
that's what I love about being British.

The Golden Jubilee unites the nation in celebration,
the Union Jacks fly at full mast,
the atmosphere filled with happiness and jubilation.
A tribute to British culture has emerged before our very eyes,
deep down we're proud of being British,
our love endures and never dies,
and that's what I love about being British!

Fine Buliciri

The Queen Mother

So, another old lady has died today
The Queen Mother of Britain, what can I say?
Her titles told us why she was grand,
There was always the smile and the wave of the hand.
The clothes and hats in distinctive style
Ready to chat and linger awhile.
From those in the know, we heard the stories
Of love and laughter recalling past glories.
In private a family like any other
Beloved granny, caring mother.
Their loss the same as any other one
To her subjects she was just the Queen Mum.
Regal, royal, and gracious, they say
Privileged, cosseted in every way
But that is because she was a Queen
Like many before, they were there to be seen.
Life will go on without her here
Her influence gone, it will be clear
Elizabeth II will shine like a star
To bloom in her own light, how long, how far?
We will miss the old lady with love of corgis
Horses and gardening and racing glories.
St Peter in Heaven will welcome her in
Will place in her hand a Dubonnet and gin,
With a welcoming smile, say 'Come in Liz,'
One only King here, the royalty His.

P Evans

THE BRIGHTEST LIGHT

When I heard that you'd gone into God's garden of rest,
That your soul He had placed with the very best.
My heart filled with sadness to lose a friend,
Whose outstretched hand she was willing to lend.
Her willingness to lend a listening ear,
Brush away my confusion, help me see things so clear.
Though I'm sad at your passing, I'll send up a prayer,
You were one in a million, in this world that's rare.
So I'll let you go now so you can sleep,
Before joining God's flock of faithful sheep.
As you pass through the gate of glory so bright,
I will search in the heavens for the brightest light.
And when I have found you on a night that is clear,
Then I'll lift up my head and shed a joyful tear.
So sleep now my friend in God's warm caress,
Sleep now my friend in God's garden of rest.

S M Wilkinson

REFLECTIONS ON THE QUEEN MOTHER AT THE LYING-IN-STATE

The rarest diamond in the World
Was not upon the crown
But lay beneath in coffin draped
A Queen of World renown.

She was not born of regal line
But destiny held sway
Her life was set the throne to take
And rule Empires of the day.

A Monarch with a human touch
She loved the common folk
When dreadful War besieged our land
She helped to lift their yoke.

She mixed with Kings and lived with wealth
But everyone she loved
Oft times good things were done by stealth
She ruled with a fine kid glove.

Each one she met felt special then
With this gentle smiling face
All would succumb to her great panache
Her charm and noble grace.

Young and old felt quite at home,
In the presence of this Queen
With pensioners to children small
She was delighted to be seen.

Her spirit, fortitude and love
For the people of this land
Sustained us all through War and Peace
To those unnumbered as the sand.

The sparkle of the Koh-i-Noor
Is a beauty to behold
But we were blessed by a diamond more rare
A Queen with a heart of gold!

Mollie D Earl

MY FATHER

My father was a miner
At a tender age he went
Beneath the ground
To cut the coal
To help the family rent

Many dangers he met there
He survived each and all
Until the day
The mine blew up
But he escaped the fall

It was then he decided
He must leave that industry
Once in London
Then back home
In the building industry

In South Wales he settled down
And there he met his future wife
Through the hard times
And the good times
He lived an exemplary life

He worked hard, had no vices
And loved his wife and family
He had two boys
And then three girls
All brought up properly

He may not have achieved fame
In the roll call, but to
His children and
Grandchildren he was
The best father of all.

Terry Daley

MARCH 10TH

Mother's Day is here, 10th March
Those special words sent touch my heart
Maybe presents for all of us
But I am not bothered about any fuss
Just to know that they still care
Knowing also our love we can share
The loving words brought this day
Start to take my breath away
Hope your children think of you, the way
                             mine think of me
Because they will always remain, a very
                             special part of me.
        You are always in my heart
                             Mum.

Anne Davey

MY SPECIAL FRIEND

My friend, my very dear friend,
Who, as spring turned into summer
And dark clouds rolled away
With the sun brought warmth,
Laughter, joy and happiness
And moments to treasure.
And whatever autumn, winter
Or future seasons bring for you
Or me, you will always have a
Special place in my heart
And I hope you will always be
My friend, my very special friend.

Diana Daley

SPIRITS LIVE ON

Growing up you were always there
When I was sick you provided my care.
I never showed how thankful I was
Until this day and that's because . . .
Spirits live on and I think you do
I mean when I say 'I love you.'

I never realised and now it's too late
Didn't say how I felt, myself I hate.
If only you knew how important you are
Even though you've gone to a place afar.
Spirits live on and I think you do
I mean when I say 'I love you.'

Laura Linfield-Brown

MY DAD

Dad is another name for strength
'Edward John Healy' is my daddy,
When he was young,
He was a bit of a lad,
He liked a beer or two,
A drop of whiskey or two,
He worked for British Leyland Cars,
Now he's in our garden digging veg.

'Edward John Healy',
He's my dad,
And he cares,
Dad, you're the King of Hearts,
And I,
'Marion Ann Healy' love you,
And if you need me,
I'll be there,
Dad,
I love you,
You're forever in my
Heart
I'll never depart
I love you,
Dad . . . 2002

Marion Healy

MY LOVING BRIDE

You are the apple of my eye,
Your youth and beauty will never die,
My love for you will never fade,
You are my woman
A beautiful babe,
You are the love in my heart,
From you, 'Joyce',
I'll never depart,
For 'Joyce'
I love you so,
And my love from you, I'll never go,
I'll never leave your side,
'Joyce'!
You're my loving
Bride . . .

Eamon John A Healy

A Golden Jubilee Riddle

Riddle a riddle by me,
for Queen Elizabeth II Golden Jubilee.
Fifty years she wore a crown,
her loving name has great renown
and she still is a good-looking beauty.

Riddle a riddle by me,
As Ambassador for Britain with eloquency.
she travelled world-wide for a while,
with friendly handshake and a smile,
spreading lots of peaceful love and harmony.

Riddle a riddle by me,
Buckingham Palace had a rock concert to see.
Fans flocked to see it by the score,
pop idols sang the songs we all adore,
and fireworks cascaded into twinkling stars merrily.

Riddle a riddle by me,
The crowds cheered our beloved Queen whole-heartedly,
St Paul's Cathedral bells did ring,
a sweet choir harmoniously did sing,
and Elizabeth was blessed by Archbishop of Canterbury.

Riddle a riddle by me,
Such spectacular street processions I did see.
A festival of songs, butterflies and flowers,
I watched it on my television for hours,
with glass of wine to toast the Queen so lovingly.

Joyce Dawn Willis

MOTHER'S DAY

Dear Ma,

Good morning to you on Mothering Sunday
A day for relaxing, a lovely fun day.
But soon in the kitchen preparing the meal.
I can't help thinking you have got a raw deal.

On returning I'll do what your dear heart wishes
I will sweep and I'll dust
I will even do dishes.

I hope these gifts will ease the pain
A swig of the bubbly could make you feel sane.

So for all your years of selfless devotion
The time has come for a big promotion.

Your stirling qualities make me feel inferior
So I think I'll promote you to Mother Superior.

Sue Wichman

Bob

It will take me a while to remember
To make just one cup of tea.
Or lay just one place at the table,
Not two, as it used to be.

It may take me a while not to call you
As if you were sat in your chair
And expect you to answer 'Alright Doll!'
'Til I recall you are no longer there.

It may take me a while to stop crying
When I think of the life we once shared.
When with only a glance you would tell me
Just how much you really cared.

It may take me a little bit longer,
To not see your face everywhere,
I can still feel your love all around me
And wherever I turn, you are there.

It will take all my life not to miss you,
Your smile, and your gentle way,
To forget I can no longer tell you
How happy you made every day.

It may take a while for the future
To hold any meaning for me
For the past is all I can think of
And how life with you used to be.

Betty Buckle

Mum

A mother's work is never done
I've often heard it said.
There's no wage for a mother
She's paid in love instead.

You may think your words unheeded
That your efforts are in vain,
But when your children smile at you
They're loving you again.

Their laughter shows they're happy.
Bright faces, thanks to you,
Reflect the love you've given them,
Such payment is your due!

Margaret Thomas

MY HUSBAND, ROY
(6th October 1930 - 21st May 2002)

Not just a husband, we shared everything
Lover, companion, all year was spring
Because of the age gap, we knew he'd go before,
Leaving me on the Earth to think of that door
Which one day he will open for me to walk through
But many tomorrows may still come for me
I can carry on living, I can't set him free

The Earthly time we shared was ours
We did not need demonstration and flowers
From the start we just 'clicked' with our love and desire
Needing each other we ignited one fire
Which will never burn out, the embers will glow
Until the heavenly time comes and again we'll both know
How true was the heart and how slender the thread that kept us apart

Remembering the first time you kissed me
May lighten my heart and sorrow may flee
The warmth of our love somehow still sets me on fire
Is it you from somewhere wanting to share my desire?
Yes, it must be, for only we two could ever feel
Such mutual love, so deep and so real.

Celia Taylor

FOR DAVID MY SON

You've always been there, stalwart and strong,
Trying to right anything that went wrong
Loving me always, one hundred percent
Just knowing I'm happy, makes you content
You are so solid like the Rock of Gibraltar
Yes even in bad times you didn't falter
You stood all my nonsense, my crying and pain
And helped me get back on the right path again,
Yet still you continue giving and caring
About me and checking on how I am faring,
The depths of your love, no one could measure,
What did I do to deserve such a treasure?

Doreen Walters

BEN

Ben wants to play, his mum says 'No,
Your bedroom's a mess, some toys must go.'
'My friends are out playing, look out there.'
'Ben move yourself, don't sit and stare.'
He went to his room, tears stinging his eyes
I'll tell Mum I've done it, I'll tell her lies,
He put on his shoes and ran out of the gate,
'Come on lads, I'm sorry I'm late.'
Off they all went to play with Dean's ball,
Ben didn't hear his mother call,
Ben played for hours, he was hungry after that,
So home he went, at the table he sat,
He shouted his mum, there was no reply
So he helped himself to some apple pie.
Still no mum, where could she have gone?
He went back outside, Ben shouted to John,
'Have you seen my mum, do you know where she is?'
John's mum ran over, she gave Ben a kiss,
Ben looked confused, 'What's happened to my mum?'
'I've got some bad news, come with me, son.
Your dad's coming soon, he'll take you with him.'
Ben cried out loud, 'I want my mum.'
John's mum sat by Ben and held him close,
'Your mum died, Ben, she took an overdose.'
Ben didn't understand, he couldn't speak a word,
'My mum wouldn't leave me, it's not true what I heard.'
'Your mum was sad, she couldn't cope anymore
She left you a note, it was on the floor.'
Ben read the note, he cried and cried
'I didn't mean not to help, Mum, I wish I hadn't lied.'
'It's not your fault Ben, she tried her best,
She didn't want to leave you, Ben, she's at rest.'
Ben's dad came in, he looked at his son,
He hadn't seen him for three years, what had he done?

He walked out on Ben's mum, love had been lost,
She'd struggled on with Ben and look what it cost?
Ben's left with no mum, he has no wife,
She was so alone, she took her life,
He walked up to Ben, they cried together
'I'll never leave you again Ben, never, ever.'
He kissed his dad, his face was sad,
'I miss my mum now, I'm just glad you're my dad.'

Those words made me cry, I held him so tight,
I couldn't let him go, I held him all night.
'I'll do you proud son, at the end of the day.
It's all my fault, the price we have to pay.'
The funeral came, Ben couldn't see through his tears,
He's gone through a lot in his nine years.
Six roses Ben sent, six words he wrote.
They read, 'Mum, I'll always keep your note.'

Elaine Chaplin

DAUGHTERS OF MINE

Be honest with yourselves my dears
And loyal to your friends
Don't talk too much, for words, as such
Will oft' times cause offence
But talk enough, and ride rebuff,
Rely on your good sense.

For you are everything to me
Nay, everything and more,
Worth every breath I've ever drawn,
Every ache and flaw.
And every time I look at you
My heart just fills with pride,
Too small am I to be your sky
So I stand by your side
Forever
In your shadow
Ever watchful to your cause,
For you I stand
You have my hand
In darkness, light and gauze.

I cannot tell you what is right
For I only know what's wrong,
Seek answers in the times that pass
In solitude and throng,
Though I may guide 'tis you decides,
I'll always love your song.

For the truth my dears is wisdom dies
And love has many forms,
It's how we treat those things we meet
That keeps us safe in storms,

Remember well
Tomorrow always follows from today,
Just be your best
For all the rest
'Tis naught but life they say.

In smiles and tears remember
From the good we see the bad,
And through it all my love stands tall
I'll always be your dad,
At the pinnacle of privilege
My gift to see you grow
Two angel souls from Heaven sent
Your smiles are all
I know.

Steve Myers

THERE ARE ANGELS

Feel I've found you
A piece that can never be mine
Could I imagine you then
See your smile, hear your giggle
Fade me back in time till then
Please Lord just want to there be
Her as she was: a lovely child
Wanted to see where she began
And so continues now for me
There are Angels, for each there are
Angels for us all on Earth
For each a special star
Wish to stand and watch you play
To see the joy in you: simplicity
Know you completely if I could
Was here your life began
So much will never be mine
But fades and around me again is this time.

A C Dancer

A MIGHTY MAN
(In memory of Pastor E McCullough)

A guiding hand, a shining light
Arms of comfort, words that delight
A champion of faith, a spiritual warrior
Always putting yourself last
For your family and church

Even when weak, still you praised
Praying for others, you never once ceased
Your love touched afar
Your wisdom changed many
Even now you are gone, your ministry lives on

You really were one of a kind
A prince, a servant, a mighty man
You inspired many, you changed us all
Everyone will miss you, 'til we meet once more
We pray we will have your passion
We pray we will have your desire
But most of all and most importantly
We pray we all meet you in the morn.

Steven Hunter

My Son

So much beauty
So little time
So much to pass on to you
So much knowledge
Yet I know so little
So many years
Yet I have done so little
So much love
So hard to share
My little one
Forgive me if I tend to smile when I look at you
For I want things to be right for you
I want your life to be good
I need to give
I need to share
I need to show you how to look
I need to pass on what I have learnt
For I have only one purpose
To make your life better than the one I have lived
So much kindness in my heart
Yet sorrow in my soul for I know deep in my heart
I have failed, for I need to see the
Sunrise, a few more than I have left
But there will never be enough, springs,
Summers, autumns, or winters to share
To teach
To learn
To care
To love
Or to stand on this Earth holding your
Hand or to see your smile or hear your voice
My son I want to be forever by your side.

K Vaughan

WE WILL REMEMBER THEM

Two pretty girls, more precious than pearls,
go for a stroll, both happy young souls.
Proudly exhibiting their favoured team's shirt
the bold red of United - Manchester.
Shop window gazing, admiring nice things,
a skip through the park, and a go on the swings.
Smelling the flowers, as they look round and stare
enjoying the freedom of August's fresh air.
Chatting and laughing, as most buddies do.
Not knowing the danger, each step led them to.
The pals never realised, how time goes so swift.
'Twas getting late, and they'd both been missed.
The police were informed, they started to search.
Time passed so fast, the days were soon numbered.
News spread o'er land and sea, shocked folk prayed hopefully,
trusting a miracle would happen, to make their hearts gladden,
but that was not so, they were regrettably saddened.
A foolhardy, presumptuous, pretentious twit,
overwhelmed by a childish 'common error'.
'An own goal', he should have laughed off,
instead let it breed, to corrupt his own soul.
So seeing red, caused an explosion of anger, prompting him
to pour his revengeful venom on innocent, helpless girls.
(Their two smiling faces, are imprinted on all caring minds).
God bless Holly and Jessica. Your memories are forever.

Peggy Johnson

MY GRANDPARENTS (1999)

I'll never forget my grandparents,
No matter how old or wise.
They're always there to protect me,
Under the stormy skies.

When I need some time to think,
To unravel my problems and cry,
With open hearts they'll greet me,
And will never criticise or lie.

Whatever the trouble, they'll always be there,
No matter the place or time.
With all my heart I'm glad to say,
That my grandparents are mine.

Laura Somerville

MY MOTHER

Mum made all my coats and dresses
Carefully combed and brushed my tresses
I know she loved me very dearly
But Mother never kissed me

Mum was keen on speech and manners
They were sixpences - not tanners
Say 'Good morning' - not 'Hello'
That's the path I had to go
Whether it be sun or rain
Always use the person's name
But Mother never kissed me

My friends were always welcomed there
Table set with tempting fare
Read aloud to me each night
Mum always taught me wrong from right
But Mother never kissed me

Packed my lunch when off to school
An apple, orange, was the rule
When away from home *she missed me*
But Mother never kissed me

Now Mother's joined the higher plane
Cast aside the mortal chain
I'd not have changed her for another
I loved her so - my caring mother
My happiness will be complete
If and when some day we meet
Mum will kiss me!

Betty Mai Challinor

OVER THE RAINBOW
(For Holly Wells and Jessica Chapman)

From dancing fountains to silent streams,
Happiness to empty dreams,
From laughter and joy to sadness and sorrow,
No hope anymore to live for tomorrow,
From smiling faces and football shirts,
To tragedy, grief and deepest hurt,
We have adults to blame,
For this heartache and shame,
Who took away all precious things,
That the lives of these little girls did bring,
The right to live, to grow and love,
To play and run as the sun shone above,
Two beautiful children, that's Heaven's gain,
Those left behind in a sea of pain,
Holly and Jessica always together
May they play and stay this way forever.

Kelly Pidwell

A Mother

A mum is worth the having - a mum is much adored
A mum is who one turns to - if the time she can afford
The time to hear what annoys you - or what pleases you instead
It's a mum who gives the guidance - when you wish to get ahead
A mum too is a partner - a partner who is shared
A mother is the cook too - when a meal is to be prepared
A mum is a special present - from He who dwells above
There is nothing that is finer - than to know a mother's love
A mother is the referee - to help a 'war' to cease
A mother is the saviour - who can bring about a peace
A mother is forever - until she is short of breath
A mother remains within you - even separated by her death
A mother disappearing - will leave an empty hole
But she'll remain to fill it - because she's left a loving soul
A soul that's not forsaken - although you're far apart
A mother will be within you - within a broken heart
You will recall her values - you will remember charms
You will always wish to hold her - clasped within your arms
There will come those moments - when you will feel the loss
Be brave and face those moments - if only and because
That mother whom you loved so - has left you with the hope
That you had learned from she - how a mother needs to cope
Of course that painful heartbreak - that you may try to hide
Is because you love her - and you feel your mum inside
Find the strength to hold on - grasp it like a glove
Then you too will be a mother - who understands a *mother's love!*

John L Wright

BEST FRIEND
(For Selena)

Forever, behind your selfless smile,
is a friendship that is so strong.
In you I seem to find my strength,
it's you who helps me to carry on.

Through the times that seemed so troubled,
times that seemed so hard -
it's you who would pick up the pieces
and mend my broken heart.

Words don't seem to describe us,
the way we've always been.
so many years of friendship -
it doesn't tend to seem.

So if I ever leave you behind or
in my shadow for a while,
don't worry my dear friend - I'll
soon be back for a glimpse of your smile.

Laura O'Rourke

TOGETHER FOREVER
(Holly and Jessica - 'God bless you both')

Two little girls went out to play
But weren't seen again from that day,
Someone whom they must have known
Took advantage of them being alone.
Instead of being treated kind
Sinister thoughts were on the abductor's mind.
So many people, have shed lots of tears
For those beautiful girls of such tender years.
In life, they were friends full of play,
Now in death, together they lay
A merciless killing, the question is - why
These two little girls had to die?
It's all so very, very sad,
Our hearts go out to their mums and dads,
From Holly and Jessica, you are torn apart
But they'll always be there,
Safe in your hearts.

Sheila Buckingham

RUBY WEDDING ANNIVERSARY

Was forty years ago I took your hand,
And on it I placed a golden band.
When asked the question
You said 'I will.'
You know, my dear, that was a thrill.

Our life together has been so grand.
It makes me glad I took your hand.
You certainly know how to ring my bell.
I hope it's great for you as well.

You have cared for me all that time.
Have kept me fed and free from grime.
No man alive could ask for more.
That is why my dear, I you adore.

Peter Englefield

MY MOST PRECIOUS FRIEND

If I had a penny for the times you show you care
I would be worth a fortune, an absolute millionaire
You are precious beyond being, a friend who never strays
Not only at the good times, you're there through darker days
One word and I feel better, it's as if you can just tell
I'm sure God picked you carefully to be His wise Angel
Someone who gives their love so free
Someone who really cares for me
You'll never know the joy inside
I can be me, I need not hide.
Dear Tracey, I hope the love I give back to you
Means as much when you too are blue
More than a friend, a sister in my heart
You've always been there from the start
I hope that in your heart you know
I'll always love you wherever we go.

Sue Starling

LEAN ON ME

Mike is deaf, and could hear no more
The telephone or a knock on the door
Until one day his life was enriched
With Flint, with whom he is bewitched
She's gentle, always by his side
To tell him sounds, his constant guide.
Flint was selected from many breeds
To match with Mike, to meet his needs
The last two years the bond has grown
She's done much more than answer the phone
Flint is accompanying Mike now on his talks
She gets rewarded with treats and long walks
Raising money for hearing dogs is their aim
It takes so much to rescue and train.
Their picture on leaflets, Crufts, and in the press
Has made them famous, Flint deserves no less
For the work she's doing day by day
Carry on the good work, is what we say
Keep going Mike, to spread the word
With your devoted friend, he hasn't heard
But Flint does, and lets him know
She lifts his spirit when feeling low
The photographer captured the trust, together
Her paw on Mike's shoulder, friends forever.

Lin Sullivan

MICHAEL APOLLO RONAN CHAKOTAY KNIGHT

M is for miracle
I is for intelligent
C is for cute
H is for happy
A is for always
E is for everything
L is for life

A is for angel
P is for precious
O is for original
L is for love
L is for lively
O is for only one

R is for rascal
O is for obedient
N is for names
A is for alert
N is for nanny

C is for cheeky
H is for hungry
A is for appetite
K is for kool
O is for observant
T is for treasure
A is for angelic
Y is for youngster

K is for Knight Rider
N is for nephew
I is for innocent
G is for grateful
H is for hope
T is for temper

Michelle Knight

GRANDAD TED
(In loving memory of Edward (Ted) Bazley. He was a great dad, grandad, husband, uncle, nephew, cousin, son, brother and friend)

Grandad Ted was the best
Now he is with Nan
Now he can rest
They can catch up as fast as they can
They are both sending their love
To their family and friends
From above
So don't just cry but laugh at the end
Grandad Ted was dying of cancer
But he got on with his life. He was a good dancer
Grandad Ted was looked after by Uncle Phil
Who loved him and cared about him, and made sure he had his pills
Grandad Ted had a good life
He always loved having a joke
He has 4 kids and a wife Phyllis
He always loved a glass of rum and a smoke
He was cared for and is still loved by us
He has grandchildren, how many? 11.
He used to tell us he used to walk places and he didn't get a bus
He is not just on Earth, he is in Heaven
After his wife Phyllis died,
He made sure that the kids were all right
He was honest, funny, kind, caring, a great dad,
A great grandad, and bright
Let's celebrate his life,
Look back at the fun
Eddie, Andy and Phil, his sons
And Barbara, his daughter
He had fun with all his grandchildren,
Tash, Andrew, Claire, Kirsty, Sandie, Laura
Brian, Stacey, Shaun, Justin and Hannah
There was nothing to bore him.

He loved it when Kim went up
To see Phil and him
He had a World's Greatest Dad cup
He loved it when he had his hair trimmed
When he was on Earth he was in pain
Now he is in Heaven he won't be again
He died when he was 81
He won't be forgotten by anyone.

Tash Bazley (15)

OPEN UP

I know that you have been hurt before,
However, I cannot get in if you close the door

I will never creep back in
You need to decide whether to let me in.

Your hurts and fears are so real
I honestly know how you feel.

Lies and deception have been the game
My life has been exactly the same.

I decided not to trust anyone,
For all the anguish and pain they'd done

However, you cannot live in the past
For we have a life that passes so fast.

Look to the present and allow yourself to see
That all you need to do is to pass the key.

I'll let myself in through the barrier
And if you need me to, I'll carry you
Over the hurdle, you need to get around
I'll lift you onto solid ground.

Together we'll get through this mess
And discuss the issues that need to be addressed.

Jayne Poulter

ANCHOR BOOKS SUBMISSIONS INVITED
SOMETHING FOR EVERYONE

ANCHOR BOOKS GEN - Any subject, light-hearted clean fun, nothing unprintable please.

THE OPPOSITE SEX - Have your say on the opposite gender. Do they drive you mad or can we co-exist in harmony?

THE NATURAL WORLD - Are we destroying the world around us? What should we do to preserve the beauty and the future of our planet - you decide!

All poems no longer than 30 lines.
Always welcome! No fee!
Plus cash prizes to be won!

Mark your envelope (eg *The Natural World*)
And send to:
Anchor Books
Remus House, Coltsfoot Drive
Peterborough, PE2 9JX

OVER £10,000 IN POETRY PRIZES TO BE WON!

Send an SAE for details on our New Year 2003 competition!